Jovita Galan:
Unselfish Teacher

LOU SHERRILL

Illustrated by Dick Wahl

BROADMAN PRESS
Nashville, Tennessee

To all my former GA members and
My own grown-up GA and RA children
Karen, Stan, and Steve

© Copyright 1986 • Broadman Press
All Rights Reserved
4243-26
ISBN: 0-8054-4326-6
Dewey Decimal Classification: J266.092
Subject Headings: GALAN, JOVITA / / MISSIONS—TEXAS
Library of Congress Catalog Number: 86-6110
Printed in the United States of America

Library of Congress Cataloging-in-Publication Data

Sherrill, Lou, 1930-
　Jovita Galan: unselfish teacher.

　(Meet the missionary series)
　Summary: Examines the life of a home missionary in
Texas, including her call to missions and the work
she did there.
　　1. Galan, Jovita—Juvenile literature.
　2. Missionaries—Texas—Biography—Juvenile literature.
　3. Missions, Home—Juvenile literature.　4. Southern
Baptist Convention—Missions—Texas—Juvenile
literature.　5. Baptists—Missions—Texas—Juvenile
literature.　6. Texas—Biography—Juvenile literature.
[1. Galan, Jovita.　2. Missionaries]　I. Wahl,
Dick, 1939-　　ill.　II. Title.　III. Series.

Library of Congress Cataloging-in-Publication Data

BV2807.G35S54　1986　　266'.6132'0924 [B]　86-6110
ISBN 0-8054-4326-6

Contents

Miracle in Mexico	5
Secret Stories	11
Something New	17
School at Last	24
Time for Everything	30
Children Are Beautiful	39
Key to Happiness	48
Unselfishness Continues	56
Remember	63
About the Author	64

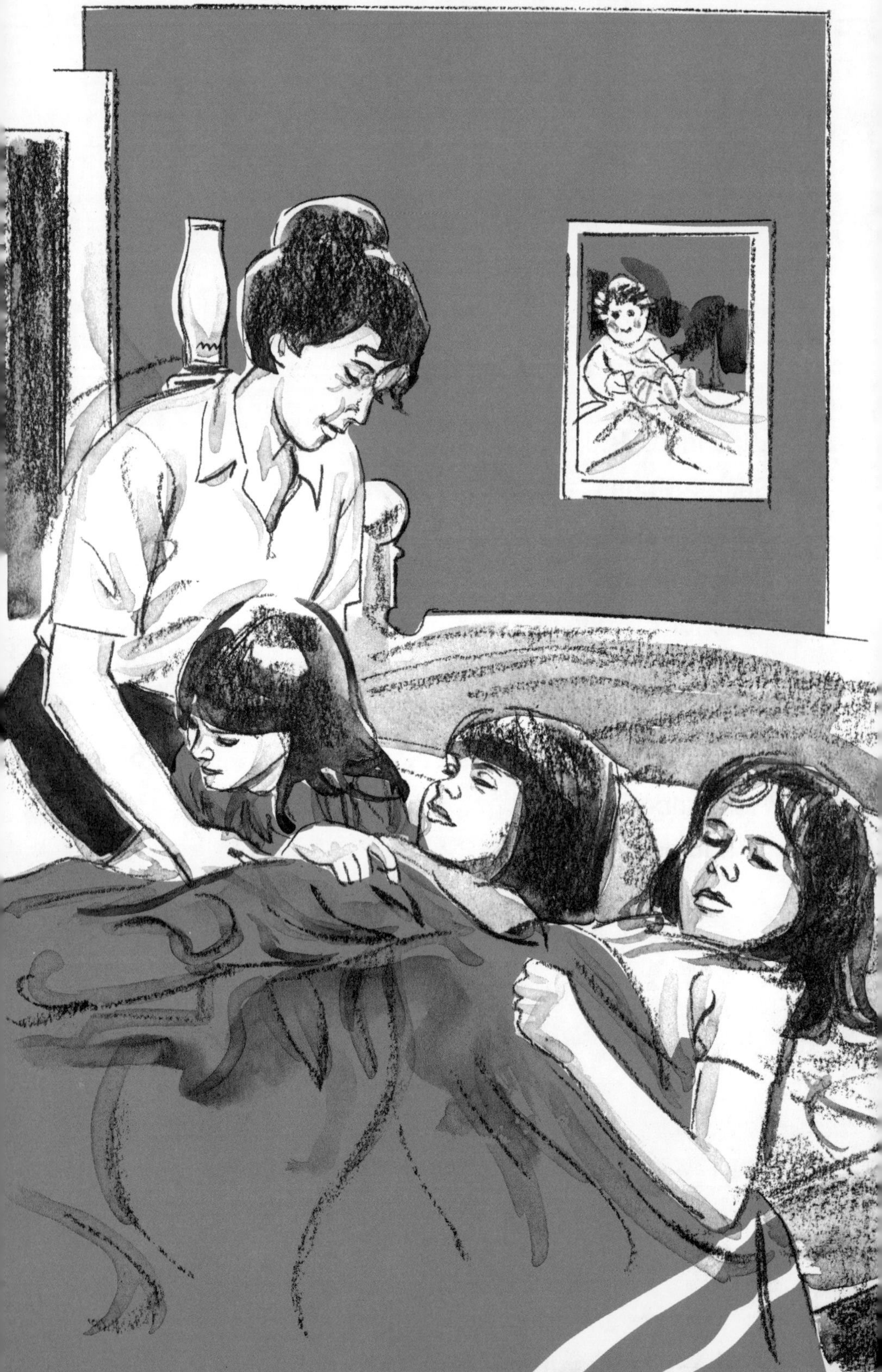

Miracle in Mexico

Dreaded Smallpox

"I can't stand anymore!" Señora Galan [sen-YORE-ah gah-LAN] said to herself over and over again. She put three-and-one-half-year-old Jovita [ho-VEE-tuh] on the bed by Esther and Delores. Now all seven children were sick. She wished she had never heard the word *smallpox*!

If only there was something she could do. In 1918 there was no medicine to give. The doctors couldn't help. Many people in Mexico were dying from the smallpox.

Señora Galan was tired and sad. Back and forth between the beds she trudged. Some of the children were too sick to eat. While nursing them, the mother would think, "I wish they could eat something. I can only give them water and lemon juice." Sometimes she had to tie the children's hands together to keep them from scratching the smallpox sores.

"Where are you going, Miguel [mee-GEL]?" Señora Galan asked.

"I'm taking these clothes to try and sell them to buy food. I'll be back as soon as I can," Señor [sen-YORE] Galan answered.

Miguel and Sara Galan worked hard to nurse their

children. They didn't have time to cry when a child died. There was too much to do for the other sick ones.

Something woke Jovita. "Father," she whispered in the night.

"It's all right. Go back to sleep." He took Esther from between her two sisters. Jovita didn't know that she would never play with Esther again. She closed her eyes and tried to sleep.

Finally, only Jovita and Demetrio [day-MAY-tree-oh] were left. One sister. One brother.

Señora Galan pushed her hair back from her face. She sighed deeply as she looked at Jovita. She could do no more.

Gently she reached down and took Jovita in her arms. She prayed, "Lord, I'm so tired! Take her—or heal her! If she lives, she will serve You."

God worked a miracle. Jovita and Demetrio both lived.

Señora Galan said many times, "I wanted each son and daughter to be a Christian and serve God."

Remembering

"Mama, where's Esther?"
"She's gone, Jovita."
"Mama, where's Isabel?"
"She's gone, too, Jovita."
"Is Delores coming back?"
"No, Jovita."

Jovita was well, and she wanted to play. She missed her brothers and sisters, especially her sisters.

She remembered their voices calling, "Jovita, come and play." She couldn't stop crying. She was sad all the time.

"How can we help Jovita?" Señora Galan asked her

husband. "She misses her sisters. Demetrio is older than she is, and, anyway, he is a brother. We must do something."

"I'll try to think of something," Jovita's father answered.

"We have one surprise for her," her mother said. "But it will be awhile before she will know about it. We must do something now."

As Señor Galan left the house, he kept thinking: "We must do something. We must do something. What can we do?"

Happiness Again

It was summertime. It was hot. The heat waves shimmered down the road.

Jovita was daydreaming. As she watched the heat waves, she thought she saw a buggy coming. Someone was in the buggy. It looked like Esther and Delores. Could it be?

No, it was just a daydream. The sadness was still there.

Just then, Jovita heard her mother calling. She turned away from her daydream. "I'm coming," she answered. She started slowly toward the door.

"Hurry, Jovita! Father has a surprise for you!"

"A surprise? What is it?"

Mother smiled. "Wait and see. I know you will like it."

Father held out a box to Jovita. She stood still. She stared at the box. "Take it. It's for you." He put the box in her arms.

Jovita couldn't open the box fast enough. Her mouth fell open. Her eyes opened wide.

"Oh-h-h, it's so beautiful! It's too beautiful to play

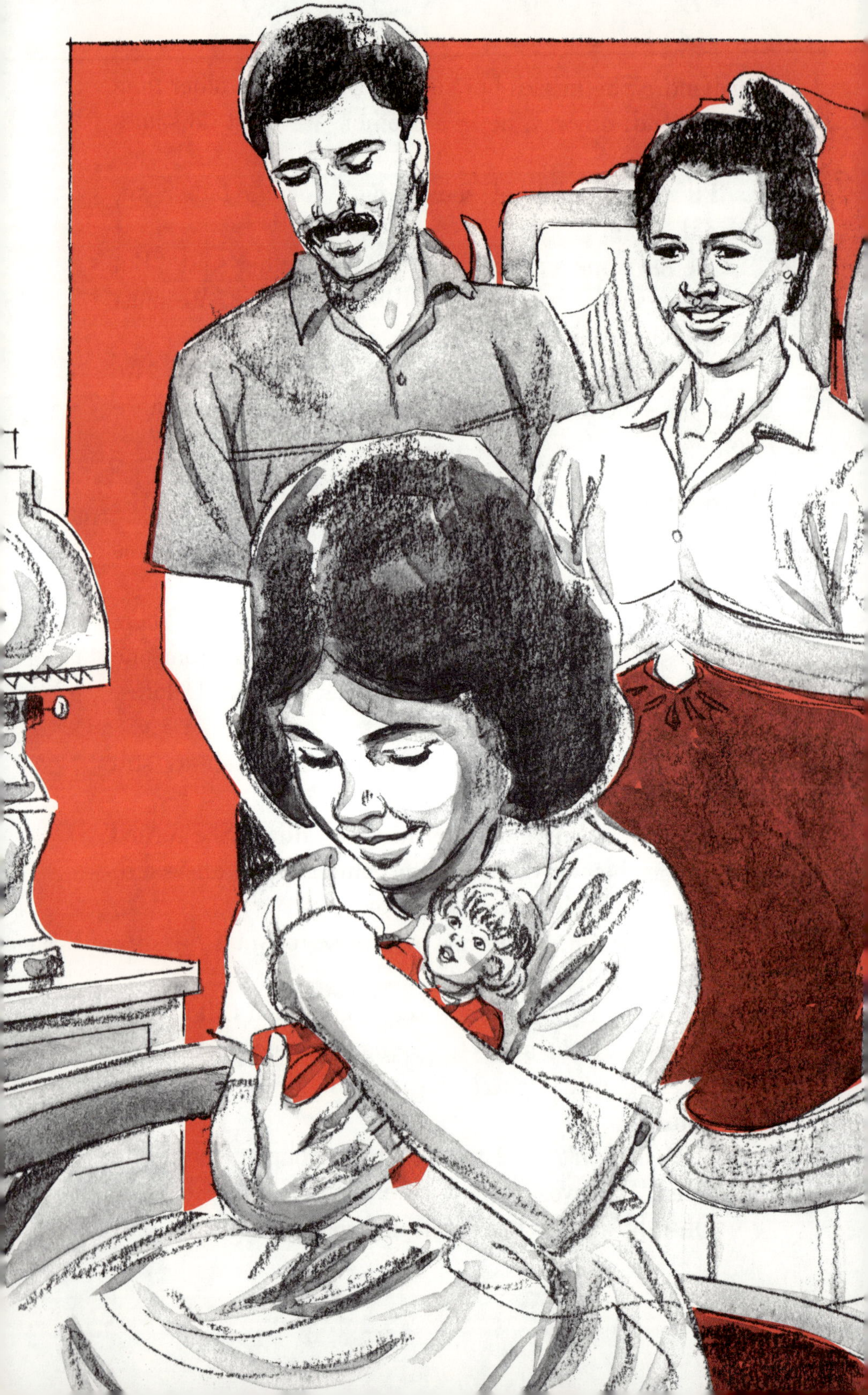

with!" She sat staring at the prettiest doll she had ever seen.

"Go ahead, take her out of the box," mother said. "She's yours. You can play with her."

Jovita carefully took the doll from the box. "I know," she said, "I will be her maestra [mah-ES-trah—teacher]."

Jovita had never had a doll before. She liked it! She spent many hours playing teacher with it. Little did she know that she would spend many years loving and teaching children.

Later, Señora Galan showed Jovita the other surprise. She showed her a baby brother named Clem.

Jovita was happy again. She loved her baby brother. He helped her not be as sad about the brothers and sisters that were gone.

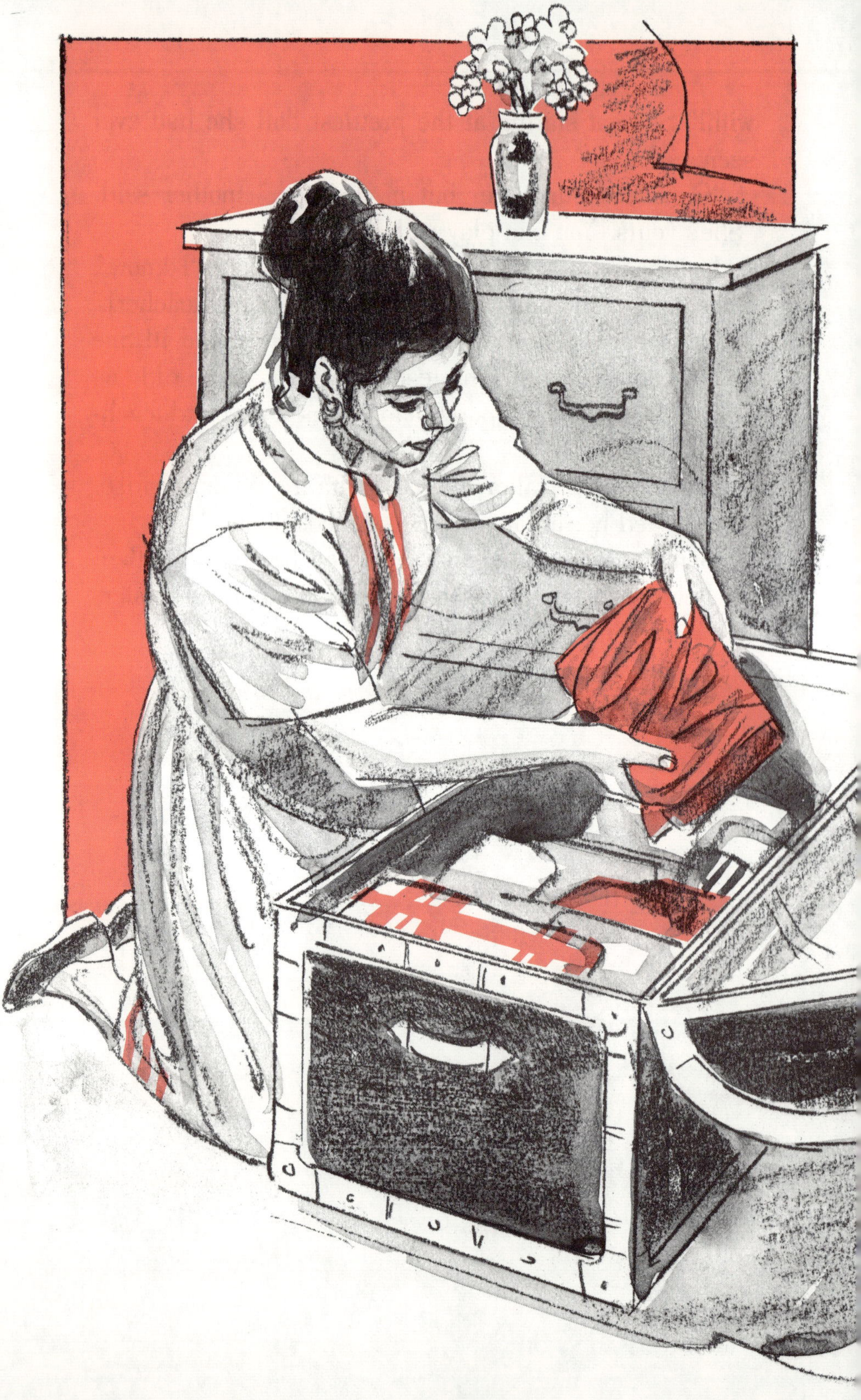

Secret Stories

From a Hidden Bible

"I don't want to see that black book anymore! If I see it again, I will burn it!" Señor Galan glared at the Bible lying on the table.

He was not a Christian. He said he was religious, but didn't attend church. He didn't want any of his family attending church either.

Señora Galan was a Christian. But out of respect for her husband, she didn't go to church. The father was the head of the house, and he didn't want anyone trying to change him.

Now Señora Galan knew she would have to be careful. Her husband had seen her Bible on the table. He didn't like it, and after threatening to burn it, he stormed out of the house.

Señora Galan picked up her Bible and hugged it close. Carefully she wrapped it in a cloth and hid it in the bottom of an old chest.

She thought to herself, "I will respect my husband, but I will try to live as a Christian in my home. Maybe, some day, he will become a Christian." She began singing softly, "What a Friend We Have in Jesus."

The children liked to hear their mother sing. They especially liked the happy song: "When the Roll Is Called Up Yonder."

They liked to hear her tell stories at night when their father was away from home.

"Mama, tell us the story about Daniel in the lion's den," Demetrio begged, "or Joseph and his brothers."

"No, I like one about girls," Jovita chimed in. "Tell us about Ruth."

Señora Galan smiled and hugged her children to her. "All right, let's lie down here on the floor, and I will tell you a story."

The children snuggled close to their mother and listened as she began, "Once upon a time . . . " She never told the children that these were stories from her hidden Bible.

Across the Border

Jovita was excited! She was eight years old and she was going to Wetmore, Texas. That was the town where she had been born on February 15, 1915.

She didn't remember much about Texas. She was only three years old when the family moved to Mexico. Now they were moving back across the border.

"This doesn't seem much like moving," Jovita said as she gave Demetrio a shove. "We don't have much to pack."

"Stop it!" Demetrio shoved back. "Remember how father had to sell a lot of our things to buy food when we all had smallpox? That's why we don't have many things to move," Demetrio reminded Jovita.

Jovita knew why they were moving. She had heard her

parents discuss this many times.

Although her father was very strict, he loved his family. He was concerned about her mother. Señora Galan could not forget the smallpox epidemic as long as they stayed in Mexico. She was sad when she thought of Isabel, Esther, Delores, Miguel, and Manuel. Besides, all her relatives lived in Texas, and she would be happier living close to them.

That was why the Galans moved in 1923 to Wetmore, Texas, and began farming. It was like starting all over again. The children helped with the farming and with housework, too.

"Jovita," her mother said, "this is your week to make breakfast." Señora Galan kept the children busy. She assigned each one to make breakfast for a week at a time. By the time she was eight years old, Jovita could do this by herself.

Jovita didn't mind. She liked cooking tortillas [tor-TEE-uhs] and cornbread cooked like pancakes.

She also cooked beans, potatoes, and chili sauce. She didn't like to cook beans. "They take too long to cook," she complained.

Her mouth watered when her mother cooked lemon pie. Señora Galan was a good teacher, and Jovita soon learned to make lemon pies, too. This was her favorite food to cook.

The children worked hard, but they found some time to laugh and play.

Time to Play

The family soon grew to include Lily, Angie, and Michael.

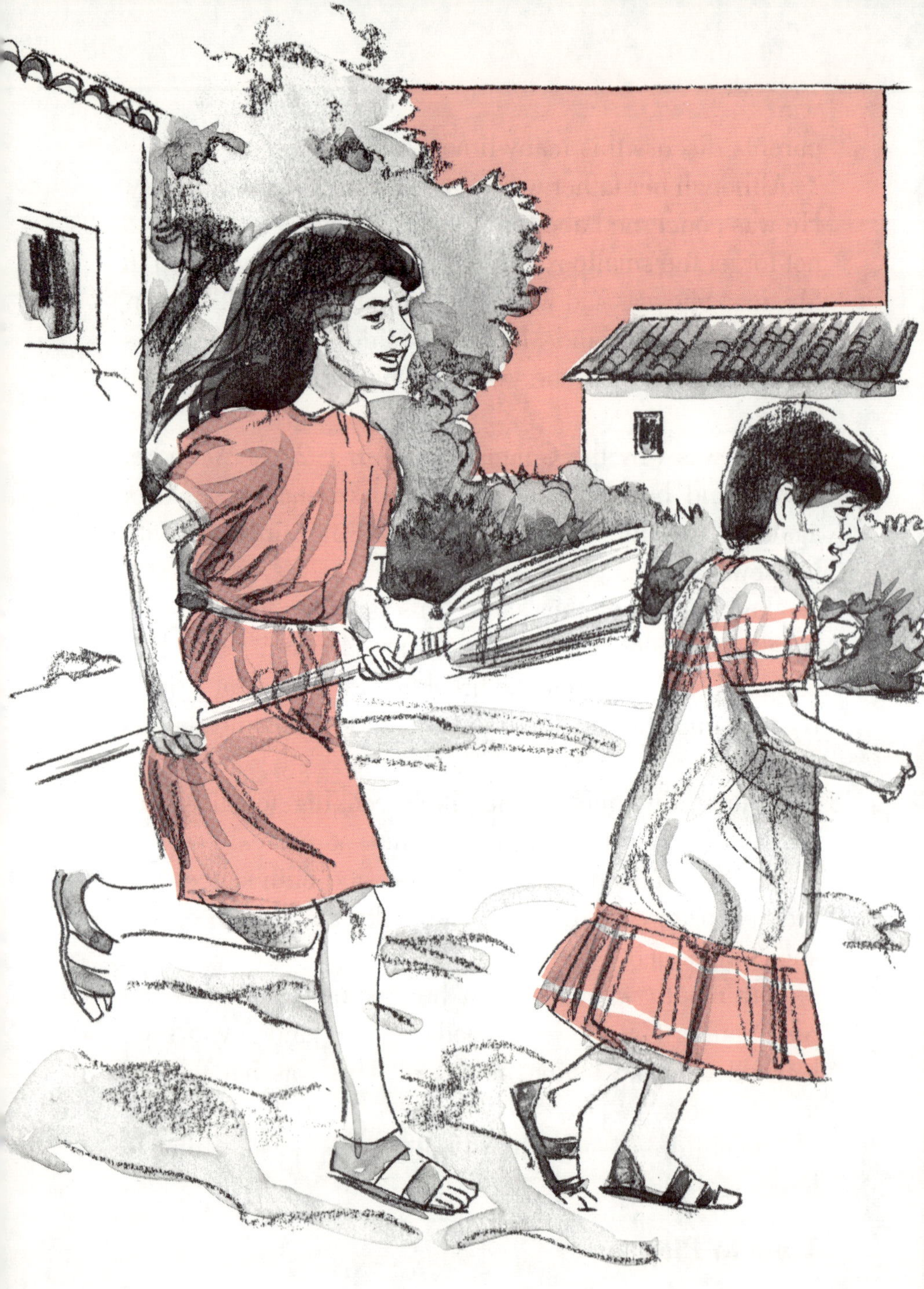

"Children, listen to Jovita while I'm gone," Señora Galan instructed as she left for a shopping trip. "Obey her. Clem, you go outside and play."

Everything went smoothly for awhile. Then Clem decided to tease Jovita by trying on one of her dresses.

"Take off my dress!" shrieked Jovita. She grabbed a broom and chased Clem through the house. She tried to hit him with the broom, but he dashed out the door. The broom caught in the screen door, and Clem made his escape.

Lily and Angie were laughing so hard that tears rolled down their faces. Suddenly, Jovita realized how funny Clem looked in her dress. She began laughing, too. She could never stay angry with him for long.

At other times, the brothers made fun of Jovita for playing with dolls. They thought she was too old for dolls. "Look! Look at the baby playing with dolls!"

Jovita didn't like it when they teased her, but she continued playing with her dolls. As she played with her dolls, she began to feel she would like to teach and work with children.

Although Clem was usually funny, he sometimes got into trouble. When that happened, Señor Galan taught all the children a lesson.

One day Clem decided that he wanted a pear to eat. The pear tree didn't belong to the Galans, so Clem sneaked along the fence looking for a tree that he could climb. "This looks like an easy one to climb," he thought. He looked around to make sure no one saw him. He shinnied up the tree and grabbed a pear. Then he slid down as fast as he could and ran away to hide. He enjoyed eating the ripe, juicy pear. It tasted good.

Señor Galan found out what Clem had done. He spanked Clem with a branch from a mesquite tree. Then he gathered the children together. He said to them, "Never go to a neighbor's and get anything that does not belong to you!"

Señor Galan was a truthful man, and he taught his children to be truthful, too.

Something New

Learning to Read

This was a special day. For a few minutes, Jovita couldn't remember why.

She stretched and yawned. It would be nice to stay in bed just a little longer. She crawled back under the covers.

Then she remembered. She was going to read in school today. She knew she could do it. Señora Galan had taught her children to read before they started to school. She had also helped them memorize verses that she called psalms.

Jovita was older than other children in the first grade. She didn't mind, though, because all the pupils met together in a little one-room country schoolhouse. She was just glad finally to go to school.

She remembered when the man with a badge came and talked with her father. He said, "Send your children to school, or you will have to pay. It's the law."

"Jovita!" Her mother's call interrupted her thoughts. "Get up and get ready for school. Don't forget to help pack the lunches."

As Jovita hurried to dress, she could smell the sausage and eggs cooking. She looked forward to eating them

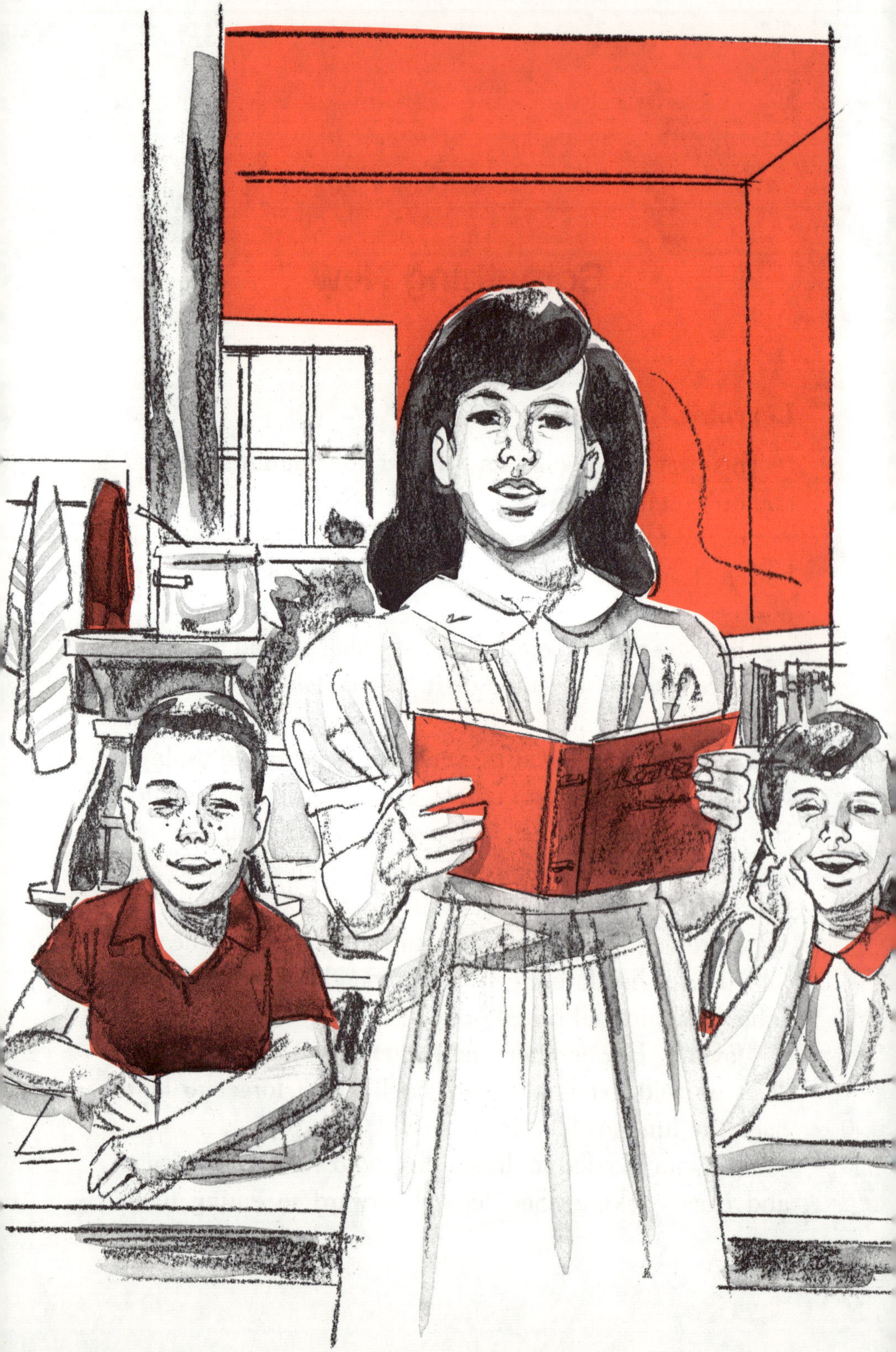

between slices of her mother's homemade bread. Señora Galan prepared sausage and egg sandwiches for the children's school lunches.

Finally, Jovita was ready to go. "Did you get your cup?" her mother asked. Jovita nodded. She would need her own cup for drinking water.

As the Galan children slipped into their places at school, Jovita looked around. She knew they were different from most of the other children. It was hard for them to make friends with the children who lived in that area where German people had settled.

"Maybe today it will be different," Jovita thought. "I am going to read."

Several children had already read, "Mary has a red ball." Now it was Jovita's turn.

She stood up and straightened her dress. She read, *"Maria tiene una bola roja* [mah-REE-ah tee-EN-nay OO-na BOH-lah RO-hah]."

Everybody laughed at Jovita. It had happened again!

Jovita's face felt hot. She wanted to run and hide. She had read in the only way that she knew—in Spanish.

As she sat down, she promised herself, "I will learn to read in English. I will read this entire book in English."

And she did.

She enjoyed going to school for two years. Then disaster struck.

Moving from Place to Place

"Come, children. Help us get things packed. We're moving today." Señor and Señora Galan were busy hurrying from room to room getting ready. As they worked, they pointed out things for the children to do.

They had waited and waited for the rains to come. Slowly, the fields had dried up. The crops couldn't grow. The Galans had to give up the farm in Wetmore, Texas, and become migrant farmers. This meant they would move from place to place looking for farm work.

First they moved to east Texas to chop cotton. All the children helped in the fields. They no longer attended school.

When they finished chopping cotton, the family packed and moved to west Texas. There the cotton was ready to pick.

After each job was done, they packed and moved again. They lived in different places all over Texas.

One day, Señora Galan said to her husband, "I am unhappy because the children have to work all day. I want the girls to go to school. We must stop moving from place to place."

Señor Galan began looking for a place to settle down. He found property in San Antonio, Texas, and bought it.

Señora Galan and Jovita were happy that Lily and Angie could finish elementary school. By that time, Jovita was fourteen years old, too old for school. She stayed home and helped with the housework.

As she was working in the house one day, she tought, "I want to learn, too. I can read. I'll teach myself!"

She began to read everything that she could get her hands on.

Señor Galan and the boys continued in migrant work for awhile. But they always managed to be at home on special celebration days.

"Hurry! Oh, please hurry!" Angie cried, pulling at Jovita's sleeve. "We're going to be too late to get a good place to see the parade."

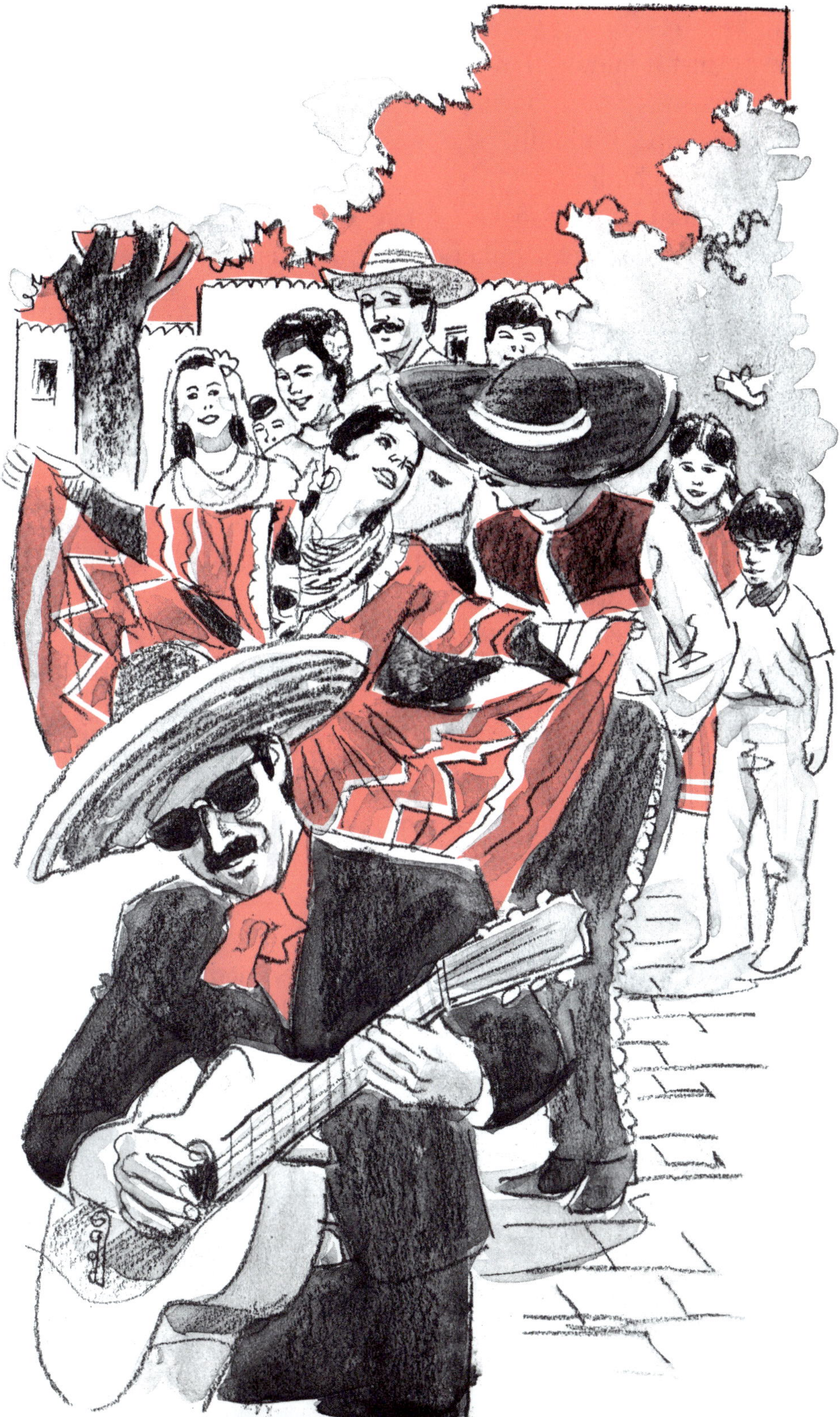

"Just a minute. I'm trying to tie Lily's ribbon. Do you have socks on?" Jovita asked. She was trying to act grown-up. Truthfully, she was just as excited as the younger children.

"Yes, I have on socks," Angie answered. "Do you have on hose? You know Father doesn't want us to go out of the house unless we're dressed right."

Lily began in a singsong voice, "No sitting in the corner with the boys, the boys, the boys!"

"Yes, that's Father, all right," Jovita thought. "And no dancing. And no movies except with an aunt or uncle."

But today was something Father did allow. Anytime there was a Mexican patriotic celebration, the Galans would be there. Señor Galan did not want his family to forget their Mexican heritage.

As they left the house, the Galans knew it would be an exciting day. After the parade, they would go to the park. Choirs would sing the Mexican anthem. People would say poems and recitations. Father would take part. They would probably buy small items from some of the many sellers. Very late in the evening, they would return home, tired but together as a family.

Bible and Church

"Do I look all right?" Jovita asked her mother.

"Yes, you look fine. See if Angie and Lily are ready to go."

Jovita helped the other children get ready. She wanted to help her mother as much as possible because her mother's brother had died. They were getting ready to attend a funeral service.

When everyone was ready to go, they started to the

church. Jovita had a funny feeling in her stomach. She had never been to a church before. She hoped she would know what to say and how to act.

She felt better as they arrived at the church. She knew many of the people. They were friendly and helpful as the family members found their places inside.

That day in church, for the first time Jovita heard someone read from the Bible. She would never forget John 14:1-6.

Later, she waited until her mother was alone. "Mama, I'm sorry about your brother. But I want to talk to you about something else. Can we talk?"

"Of course, Jovita," her mother replied. "What do you want to talk about?"

"Mama, I liked being in that mission church today. I liked to hear someone read from the Bible. I would like to go back again. May I go back again?"

Señora Galan thought for a few minutes. She wanted Jovita and the other children to go to church. But she knew how her husband felt about it. Finally she said, "I will talk with your father. If he says that it's all right, then you may go."

"Soon, Mama? May I go back soon?"

"Yes, Jovita. If your father gives his permission, you may go this Sunday."

"Oh, Mama! Thank you!" Jovita threw her arms around her mother. That sad day had suddenly become a happy day.

School at Last

Promise to Serve God

Going to church wasn't as easy as Jovita thought it would be. After she attended for awhile, Señor Galan told her not to go anymore.

Later, he let her begin going to church services again. But he didn't want her to join a church.

"Mama, I'm a Christian, now," Jovita said. "I want to be baptized and join the church."

"Now, Jovita, you know your father said no."

"But, Mama, I'm eighteen years old! Don't you think I'm old enough to decide for myself?"

Señora Galan loved Jovita, and she didn't want her to be unhappy. She thought for a few minutes before she answered. "Jovita, you say that you love God and that you want to obey Him. Prove it by obeying your earthly father. If you disobey him, how can you prove you will obey God? Think about it on your way to church."

"I will, Mama. Good-bye. I'll be late if I don't hurry."

Jovita didn't want to admit it, but her mother was usually right. She couldn't forget her mother's words. She kept hearing them over and over again as she walked to the mission.

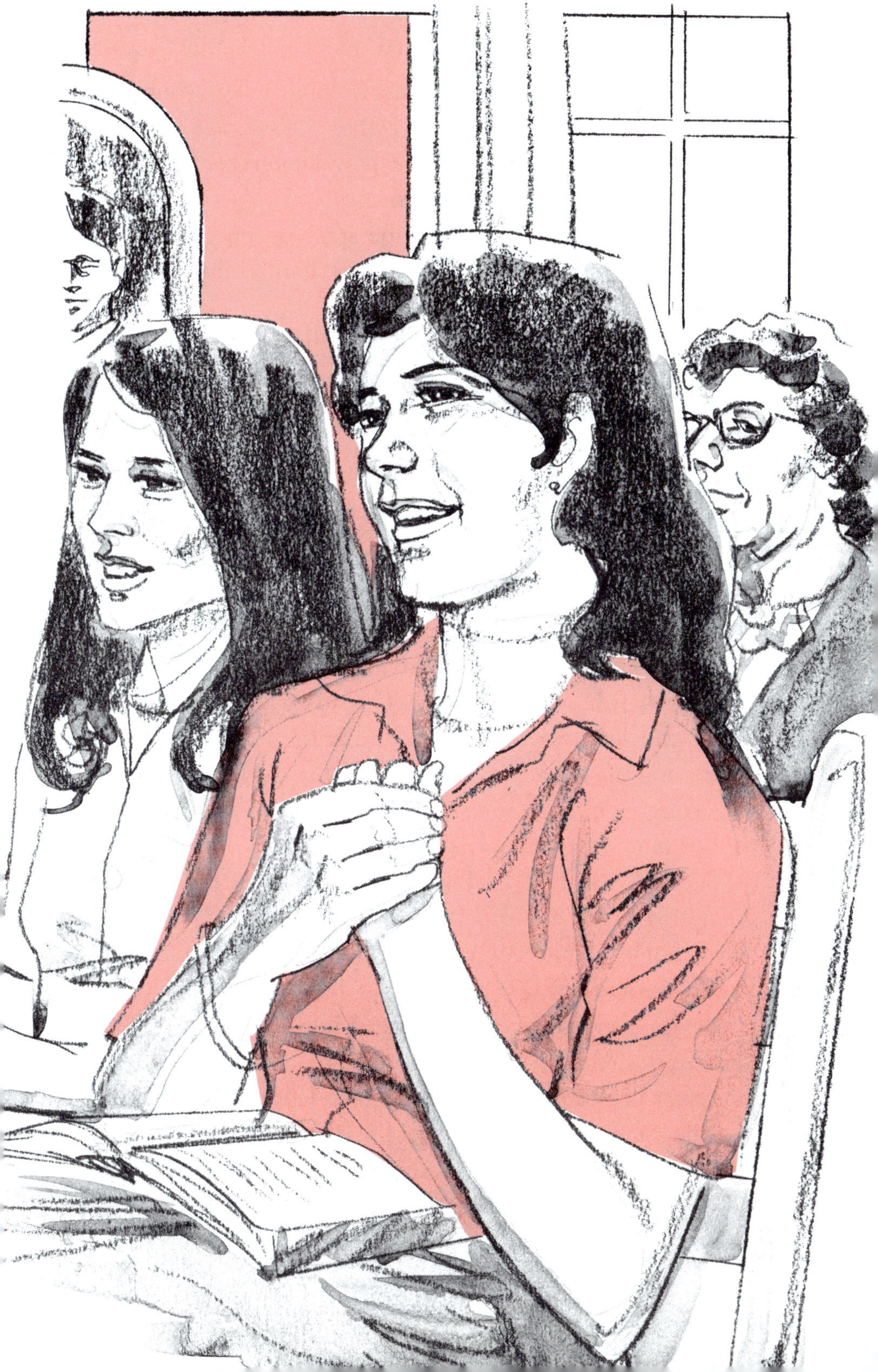

Services were held in the pastor's home. Everyone was happy as they greeted each other before the service began. "*Como esta, hermana* [COH-moh es-TAH air-MAH-nah—How do you do, sister]."

Jovita looked around until she spotted Señora Delores Diaz [DEE-ahs]. Señora Diaz had invited her to this special mission service.

Jovita could see through the door that it had started to rain. She smelled the rain and listened to it pattering against the house. Then she forgot everything else as she heard about mission work in China. She listened carefully to every word.

Something was happening that Jovita couldn't explain. Her heart was pounding. Deep inside she knew that God wanted her to be a missionary.

As she stood and sang, she meant the words of the song. "*Si Cristo conmigo va, yo ire* [see CREES-toh kohn-MEE-goh vah, yoh ee-RAY—If Jesus goes with me, I'll go]." She sang words about following the leading of God's Word and crossing the ocean or serving God at home. As she sang, she thought of her family. Most of the members of her family were not Christians.

Jovita knew that God wanted her to be a missionary. She also knew that He wanted her to serve Him in her own home. That night, she promised to serve God wherever she went.

Jovita promised God to respect her father and not be baptized yet. She would pray that her father and every member of her family would become Christians.

She smiled to herself as she thought, "We do the praying, and the Lord does the work. As long as a person lives, there's hope that he will become a Christian."

Last Chance for School

As the years passed, Jovita worked hard to help support her family. She began working as a seamstress—sewing clothes—in her home. Later she worked eight to ten hours a day as a seamstress in a factory.

Señor Galan was getting old. He was not able to work, so Jovita brought her money home.

As she worked, she continued to pray. Many of her prayers, and her mother's prayers, were answered.

Her two brothers and their wives became Christians. So did Angie and Lily.

Demetrio became a pastor. He pastored Berea Baptist Church in San Antonio, Texas, for many years. Jovita helped her brother develop this church.

One day as Jovita was sewing at the factory, she sewed a seam wrong. As she ripped out the stitches, she thought, "This is not life! I know God wants me to serve Him as a missionary. If I'm not trained, I'm not going to feel right."

She had heard about a scholarship at the Baptist Theological Seminary (Mexican) in El Paso, Texas. It was being offered for a person who wanted to prepare to serve God. But Jovita lacked a school diploma. How could she pass the tests to get the scholarship?

She thought: "Mike, the youngest of our family, is in his last year of high school. Angie is married, and Lily is working. This is my last chance! What shall I do?"

She decided to talk with a missionary friend, L. D. Moye. He encouraged Jovita. "You need to go to school," he said. "You need to get away from the family and study to prepare to do the work God wants you to do."

Jovita wanted to go, but wanting to go wasn't enough. She knew that a girl didn't leave her family without a purpose. Usually, a girl left home to get married or to begin her own home. Jovita's purpose was education.

Would her parents understand?

If they understood, could she get the scholarship?

Leaving the Family

Jovita couldn't think about anything but that scholarship. She tossed and turned in bed at night. She thought about it during the day while working at her sewing machine.

She would argue with herself: "You can't go to school and leave your family upset and angry. What kind of impression would you be giving as a Christian?"

Quickly she would continue, "I know God has called me to serve Him. I need training. I am twenty-five years old. Last year father finally gave me the freedom to be baptized. Maybe he will understand about the seminary."

"I will have faith. God will help me know what to do and what to say."

She went to her father. "Father, I need something."

"You want to marry?" he asked.

"No, Father. I need to go prepare myself for God's work. I need to go to school."

"How can you go to school?" he asked. "It takes all the money you make to buy food and clothes for the family. You would have to pay to go to school."

Jovita explained about the scholarship. "If I get it, it will take care of the cost of school. Lily is working, and she can help support the family."

Jovita and her father talked with Señora Galan. She encouraged Jovita to go.

The decision was finally made. If Jovita could get the scholarship, she could leave the family to go to school.

Jovita applied to the Baptist Theological Seminary in El Paso, Texas.

The day finally came when Jovita took the tests to try to get the scholarship. Her hands were shaking as she reached for the test papers. She was glad that she didn't have to say anything. She probably couldn't have said a word.

But she could pray. "God, You have all the wisdom. Give it to me because I cannot get it. There's no other way."

Jovita passed all the tests. She got the scholarship.

Time for Everything

Summer Missionary

Jovita struggled through her first year at the seminary. With only two years of schooling as her background, the classes were hard. But she passed.

She breathed a sigh as she hurried across the campus. She was glad the year was over. She hoped to be a summer missionary between the spring and fall sessions. She had been interviewed for the job by Dr. Loyd Corder, and she was on her way to see if she got the job.

Dr. Corder was the director of the Spanish work in Texas, New Mexico, Arizona, and California. Jovita had met him in San Antonio while she was helping Demetrio in his church. She was glad to see Dr. Corder again.

Jovita was excited. She could hardly wait to know the results of her interview. Yes! She had been accepted to serve as a summer missionary in Texas.

From that moment on to the end of the summer, Jovita was in a whirlwind of activity.

She enjoyed helping the Hispanic (Spanish-speaking) churches in San Antonio, Amarillo, and San Angelo. She helped teach in Vacation Bible Schools. She taught mission study classes and helped with GAs and RAs, the mission organizations for boys and girls.

Before Jovita knew it, the summer was over. It was time to go back to the seminary for another year of work and study.

At the end of the year, Jovita heard some bad news. The seminary was moving from El Paso.

Tears of frustration ran down Jovita's cheeks. She had studied, worked, and cried her way through two years at the seminary. She needed another year to get her diploma in religious education.

She thought, "I am preparing to be a kindergarten teacher. I need my diploma! What am I going to do?"

After spending more time in prayer, Jovita decided to attend *Centro Cultural Bautista* [bah-TEES-tuh] in Mexico for her last year of training.

When she received her diploma in 1947, Jovita praised the Lord. She said, "I feel like I am getting all of heaven. The Lord is so good. He gives us so much!"

Home Missionary

Jovita now was ready to teach kindergarten. She soon found herself doing just that—and a lot more!

She was appointed as a home missionary by the Home Mission Board and the Baptist General Convention of Texas. In September, 1947, Jovita began working in Alice, Texas.

She enjoyed teaching the kindergarten children, and the children had a good time learning. For many of the children, this was the first time anyone had taught them to obey or to say please and thank you.

They knew Jovita was their friend. She was a small woman, just the right size for bending to hear what a child

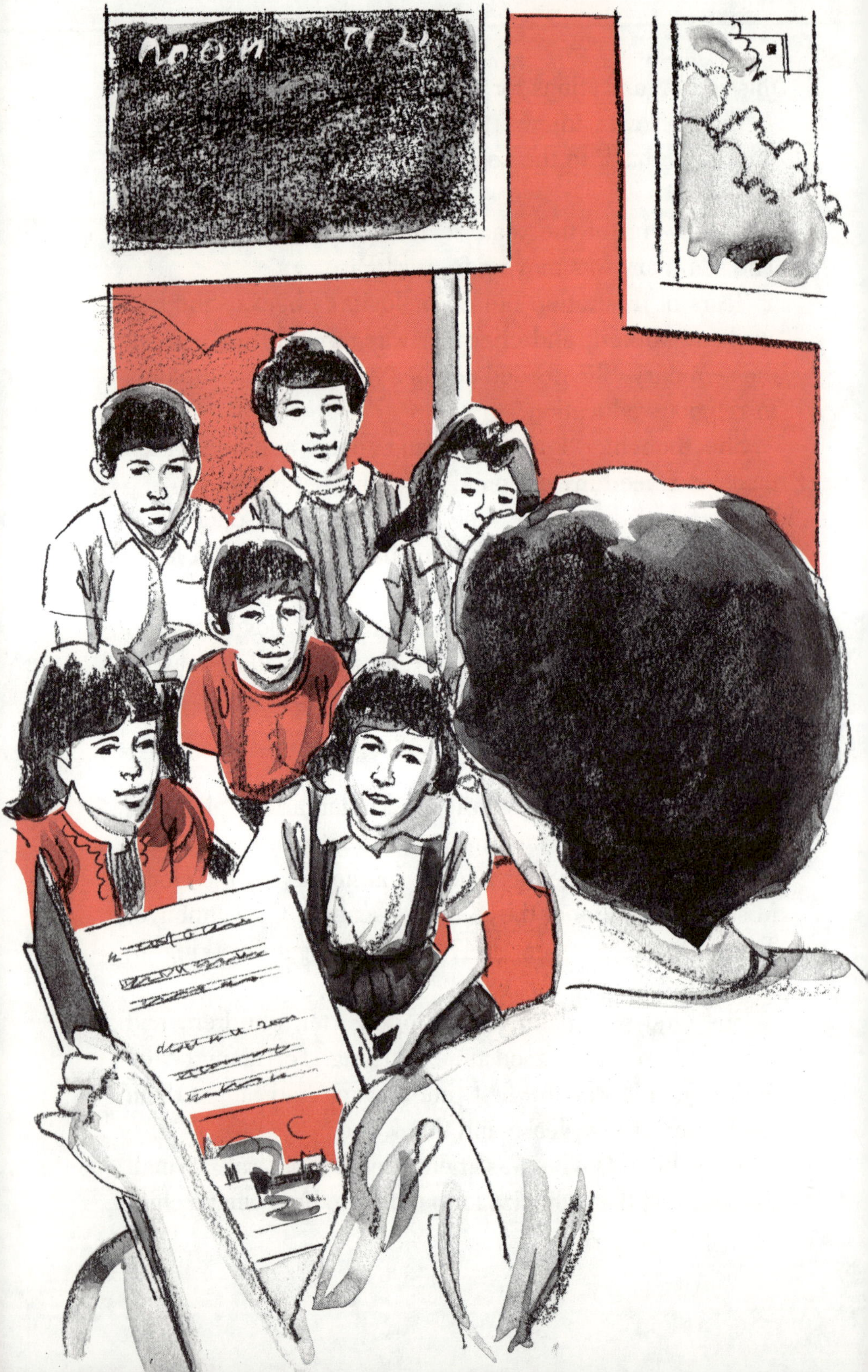

had to say. She had a round face and short, black hair. Sometimes her black eyes were smiling and gentle; sometimes they snapped as she spoke firmly to a misbehaving pupil.

Everywhere Jovita looked in the community there was something to do. Many people were sick in the hospital. No one seemed to know how to visit and care for them. Jovita taught church members how to visit.

Adults began visiting in the hospital every week. After teaching the adults, Jovita began teaching the young people how to visit.

One day Jovita said, "We can do more. I am determined to find out what else we can do."

She began a weekly radio program. Many times she took her kindergarten class and the young people to sing on the program.

The church asked Jovita to continue leading in the weekly visitation and radio program. She did, and the weeks of hard work stretched into months. The months stretched into four years.

Dr. L. D. Wood, director of missions in Texas, came to see Jovita. "Jovita, with your kindergarten class and your church activities, you have worked too hard. You need to take a year's furlough. You need to rest."

Jovita began to cry. "I guess I have done too much. But I didn't want to leave anything out that needed to be done."

"If you don't slow down," Dr. Wood warned, "you're going to be sick. You need to go to Pearsall, Texas, and work in a small church."

Jovita cried when she left Alice, Texas. She didn't want to go, but she knew that it was the best thing to do.

Again she taught kindergarten. Again she saw other things to be done.

She became GA leader for the association. She got other women to attend assocational meetings. After going to several meetings, the women discovered that they liked it!

Although Jovita was always busy, she didn't forget her family. When she could, she would talk to Angie and Lily. "You need to go to school. You need to prepare yourselves."

Angie would argue, "I can't go to school. I'm married and have a son." Later she said, "Jovita prayed my way through school."

Angie became a registered nurse and a social worker. Lily became a licensed vocational nurse. They both were active in church.

Back to San Antonio

Jovita came back to live in San Antonio. She began teaching in two kindergartens. In the morning, she taught at Antioch Baptist Church.

By one o'clock, she was eating a sandwich in the car driving across town. In the afternoon, she taught at Oriente [o-ree-IN-teh] Baptist Church.

One day Dr. L. D. Wood brought bad news. "Jovita, the Home Mission Board must cut your salary. I know you need your salary for food and your car. I'm sorry."

Jovita didn't argue with him, but she thought, "I support my family! It's not fair! Well, I'll pay the price of being hungry.

This bad news didn't affect Jovita's work. A short time later, she decided, "This kindergarten room is not pretty. The walls are ugly. I'll get some paint and get busy."

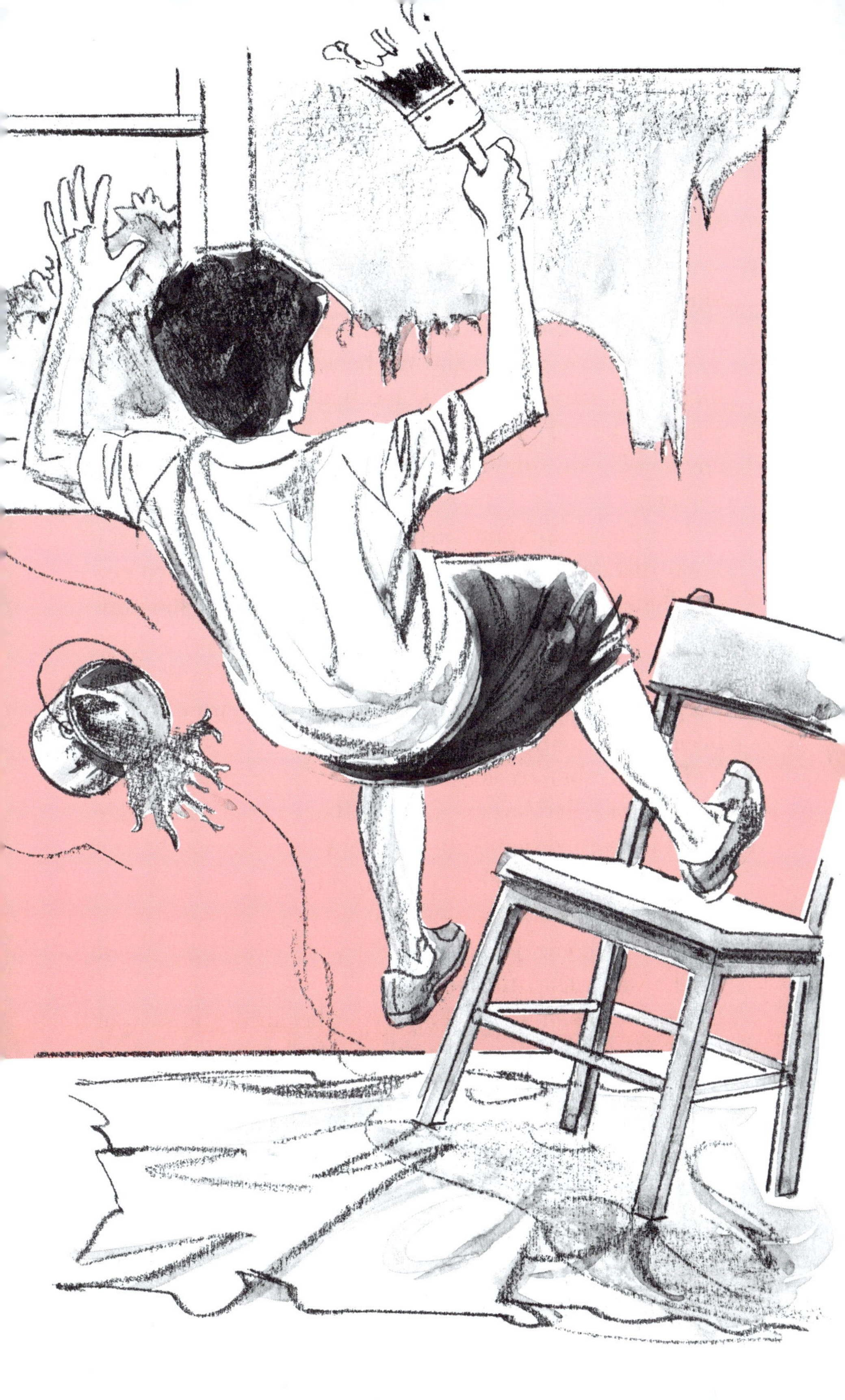

Jovita liked for things to be pretty and clean. She was enjoying painting, when all of a sudden, she fell off the chair that she had been standing on. She ended up in the hospital.

While in the hospital, the doctor told Jovita, "Your appendix has become irritated, and you also have a tumor that must be removed. You will have to go to surgery."

Thirty days later Jovita was back teaching in the two kindergartens. She soon knew that this work was too much for her. "I can't keep doing two classes. I can't do it anymore!" she admitted to herself and to the church leaders.

The Home Mission Board leaders understood. They knew that Jovita was a hard worker. They knew that she was honest about her work. They suggested that she work only at Antioch Baptist Church.

Jovita was happy about this. Because of her work many people became Christians. Jovita's kindergarten helper became a Christian.

Then another crisis came. Jovita's father, Señor Galan, had a stroke. He was taken to the Baptist Hospital. Angie and Lily helped nurse him. One was standing at the foot of his bed and the other at the head of his bed when he died.

Back at home Jovita cried, "I never heard my father say he was a Christian."

Señora Galan said, "I'm crying because I miss your father. Let me tell you something. Before he died, your father called me and said, 'I want you to pray because I believe in the Lord. About a year ago I became a Christian.'"

Jovita smiled through her tears. Once again they had prayed, and the Lord had done the work.

Iglesia Bautista Central

[ee-GLAY-see-ah bah-TEES-tah]

"You are the kindergarten teacher," the new pastor told Jovita. "You must not have the Week of Prayer for Home Missions or the Week of Prayer for Foreign Missions."

"But, that's my life!" pleaded Jovita. "I *must* tell the children about home and foreign missions." But she could not convince the new pastor.

Jovita was discouraged, so she went off alone to read her Bible. She read Psalms 3:6: "I will not be afraid of ten thousands of people, that have set themselves against me round about." And Psalms 27:1: "The Lord is my light and my salvation; whom shall I fear? The Lord is the strength of my life; of whom shall I be afraid?" These verses had encouraged her many times.

She called Dr. Wood and told him about her problem. She said, "The new pastor is making my life difficult. What shall I do?"

Dr. Wood helped Jovita to transfer to Eastlawn Chapel where she worked for a year. Then the Home Mission Board transferred Jovita to *Iglesia Bautista Central* (ee-GLAY-see-ah bah-TEES-tuh cen-tral).

At this church Jovita became director and teacher of the kindergarten along with one other teacher. She helped reorganize all the WMU organizations. She taught Sunday School and Church Training. She played the piano and directed the youth and adult choirs.

On Sunday nights, Jovita cleaned up the kindergarten rooms because they had been used for Sunday School and Church Training. She liked the rooms to be bright and cheery. By eight o'clock Monday morning she would be back at church and ready to greet the children. She taught kindergarten from 8:30 until noon.

"Don't do for the children what they can do for themselves," Jovita said. "Let them do it." They would help pass out the napkins and refreshments. They would help pick up things after activity time.

After kindergarten, Jovita often took children home. When she returned to the church, Jovita and the other teacher talked about what had happened that day. They made plans for the next day. Most important of all, they visited or called every absent pupil. Jovita also used these visits and calls to invite families to church.

Jovita would often say, "I can only visit until three o'clock. I must rest because I have a meeting tonight." If she didn't have a night meeting, she sometimes visited from the time kindergarten ended until seven o'clock at night.

Jovita liked to do extra things with her kindergarten children. She planned special programs at Christmas, Valentine's Day, and Easter. The parents came, and the children were excited and happy as they showed their mothers and fathers what they had learned.

When the circus was in town, Jovita would take the children. One teacher would be at the head of the line and one at the end of the line.

Jovita loved each child, and the children loved and respected her. She worked with many of her kindergarten pupils through their GA and RA years, through their teenage years, and even after they became adults.

"You really feel close to God among children," Jovita said. "Children are beautiful!"

Children are Beautiful

Armando (are-MON-doh)

"Armando," Jovita called, "come here. I didn't see you dry your hands." She always kept a towel hanging outside the bathroom door. She watched to see if the kindergarten children used it or not. "Did you wash your hands?"

"Oh, yes, Teacher!" Armando answered. He wanted her to know that he had washed his hands. No washing—no refreshments! That was the rule.

"Let me see," said Jovita. She took his two small hands in her hands and lifted them up to her nose. She sniffed and smiled. "Yes, I smell the soap. Good boy."

Armando Ynostrosa (ee-nohs-TROH-sah] liked to please Jovita. She had taught him so much. He remembered when he had said some bad words. She took him outside and scolded him. He never said those words again. Jovita was also the one who had taught him good manners and how to pray. From the very first day of kindergarten, children were taught to obey their teacher and be polite.

He liked to ride home in his teacher's car. The children would scramble in and crawl all over each other. One day Armando said, "This station wagon is so small, and we're so many! When I grow up and work and make money, I'm

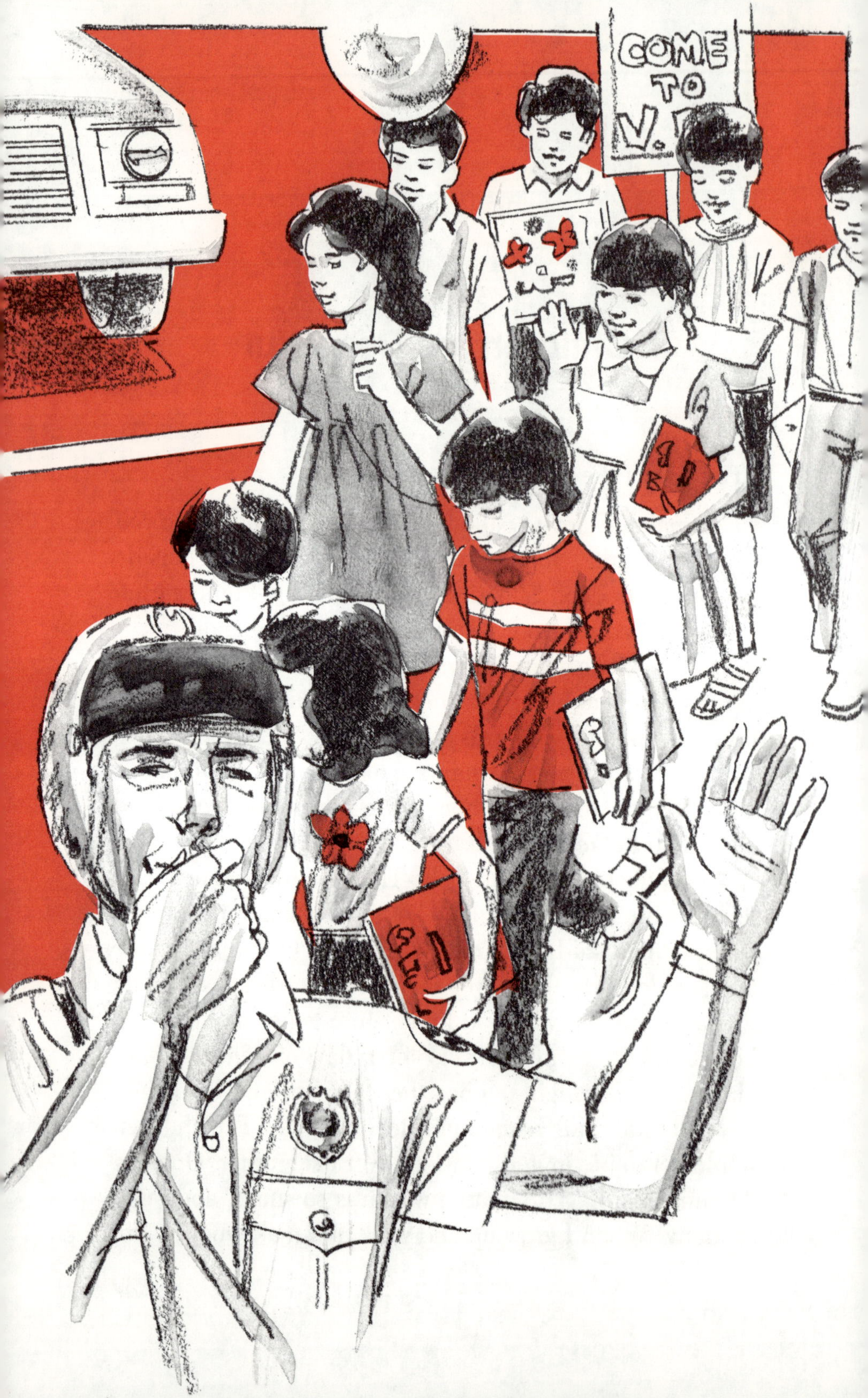
COME
TO
V.

going to buy my teacher a new *big* station wagon for all of us!"

After graduating from kindergarten, Armando was in Jovita's department for first-through-seventh graders in church. Jovita's nephew Freddie was his best friend. The two boys were in the same department. They liked to play tricks on Jovita and their mothers.

One Sunday Freddie and Armando told their mothers that they would be with Jovita. They told Jovita that they would be with their mothers. Then they sneaked out of church to play. It was fun until they got caught.

Armando wasn't always playing tricks and getting into trouble. Many times he could have played ball in the street with other boys. Instead, he went to school. During his school years, he became a musician.

As he grew older, Armando kept in touch with Jovita by writing letters. She knew that he was having a hard time in college. When she saw him at church or called him at home, she always told him, "Armando, I'm praying for you."

When he graduated, Armando wrote: "Thank you, Jovita, for the thoughtful card on my graduation. You played an important part in my life and helped me grow up in many a way! Love, Armando Ynostrosa, Jr."

Armando became a policeman and worked for the San Antonio police force. Every year he helped Jovita by directing the parade for Vacation Bible School.

When his two little girls were old enough to go to kindergarten, guess who taught them? Right! Jovita.

Beckie

"Let me help. Let me help." Beckie Marin [mah-REEN] was one of Jovita's best helpers. She was always ready to do anything she was asked.

As a child Beckie was Jovita's kindergarten pupil. She continued to be friendly and helpful as Jovita taught her in Sunday School.

After becoming a Christian, Beckie helped in visitation, Sunday School, and GA camps. She was a smart and beautiful young woman.

When Beckie moved away, Jovita missed her. She heard later that Beckie had married a fine Christian man.

Beckie continued to follow the example of her teacher. She was always looking for ways to serve God, too. She became associational Acteens director.

Beckie was told by her doctor that she had cancer. She didn't want Jovita to know, but Jovita found out about it. Beckie said, "Jovita, I know how much you love me. I didn't want to hurt you."

"You're not going to hurt me," Jovita said. "I will pray. When I pray for something, and it's God's will, it's going to happen."

At a WMU associational meeting, Jovita saw Beckie's sister. She told her, "Ruth, it hurt me so much to hear that Beckie has cancer."

"Have you heard about her surgery?" Ruth asked.

"No. What happened?"

Ruth told Jovita the rest of the story. One day the doctor had told Beckie, "You must have surgery today."

Beckie said, "Please postpone the surgery. I need to go tomorrow and lead a GA study in the association. The work of the Lord comes first."

The doctor had postponed the surgery until the next week. When he operated, all of the cancer was removed.

Beckie continued serving as associational Acteens director. She also continued learning from her beloved kindergarten teacher.

Mary Rose

"Mother," Mary Rose called to Jovita.

"I'm not your mother, remember?" Jovita reminded her niece.

"Oh, all right . . . Granny," Mary Rose said sheepishly. She sometimes slipped and said "mother" because Jovita had kept her so much when she was a baby while her mother was sick.

"Granny, teach me to play the piano," begged Mary Rose. She would not be ignored.

Jovita enjoyed teaching Mary Rose to play the piano just as she had enjoyed teaching her in kindergarten. She was a good pupil.

Jovita never had any trouble getting Mary Rose to go to church. She was a good GA member. Later she played the piano, sang solos, and became the music director. She was very active in the church.

"Granny, teach me to drive." Of course, Jovita taught Mary Rose to drive. She helped her get her driver's license.

Jovita continued helping Mary Rose as she grew up and went to the university. Jovita always prayed for her and gave her support. Sometimes she gave Mary Rose a little money when she could.

Things changed when Mary Rose fell in love.

Jovita took Mary Rose to classes in the morning. She would go back at three o'clock to pick her up. Many times Mary Rose's boyfriend would take her away from school. He almost made her miss some important tests. This hurt Jovita. She thought it was wrong.

Mary Rose asked, "Granny, why don't you love him? He says that he's a Christian."

Jovita answered, "I don't know, darling. But your grades are going down. You have stomachaches, and you are nervous. Love should make you beautiful and happy, not sad and sick. There's something wrong."

Mary Rose cried. She got sicker. She argued with her boyfriend about Jovita. Finally, they broke up.

Three months later, this man almost killed a woman.

Mary Rose came crying to Jovita. "Granny, you had a reason for not wanting me to marry him. Mama had a reason! I had a Christian testimony to lose if I had married him."

Mary Rose continued her education. She became a high school math teacher and later married.

Her husband didn't have the deep love for God and the church that Mary Rose had. They stopped going to church every Sunday and only went occasionally.

Jovita said, "I asked the Lord to watch over Mary Rose. He is going to take care of her."

Mary Rose promised, "One of these days, Granny, I'm going to get right with the Lord."

Rudy

"In that house," said the pastor, "lives a young man who used to come to church all the time. He lives with his father. They don't go to church anywhere now." The pastor and Jovita were out visiting for the church. Jovita said to herself, "I will try to visit that home and meet that young man. I knew his mother before she died, and I know his two aunts."

Later Jovita returned to the Sanchez [SAN-chess] home. While she was visiting with the aunt and grandmother, she met Rudy. "Rudy, why don't you come back to church?" she said. "We have a good group of young people. I am the leader, and I would like for you to come."

Rudy didn't promise, but on a Wednesday night the tall, skinny tenth grader came to church. The leader said, "We're happy to have Rudy with us tonight." From that night on, Rudy continued to come to church. He and Jovita became good friends.

"Rudy, how about helping me drive the station wagon on Sundays?" Jovita asked. "I get so tired driving on Sunday morning and Sunday night. I drive Monday night for YWA, Tuesday night for choir, Wednesday for church, and Thursday for GA. Will you help me?"

"Whew-w-w!" Rudy exclaimed. "I think you need some help!" He began helping Jovita every Sunday.

He helped the church in other ways, too. He became the Sunday School director.

Many times he got home late for meals on Sunday. None of his family members were Christians, and they didn't understand his love for the church. They would not save him any food to eat. "Jovita, I didn't eat today," he would say. "Come to the house and eat with us," Jovita always answered.

Rudy wanted his father and grandmother to go to church. Whe he asked them to go, they became angry. Later when Rudy told them that God wanted him to be a preacher, his father asked him to leave the house. "You don't make good grades in high school because you give too much time to your church."

Rudy went to see Jovita. He told her, "I feel that I don't have anybody in this world."

"Rudy, you have me. I am your sister in Christ, and I'm going to adopt you as my brother." Jovita turned to her mother and asked, "Mama, do you love Rudy?" "Yes," Señora Galan answered. Jovita said, "You can have a home with us."

During the day, Rudy would come to their home. He used the time to study the Bible and prepare for church.

After Rudy finished high school, he wanted to go to Howard Payne College. He had nobody to help him. "Don't worry," Jovita said. "I only have a small salary, and I support my family, but I will help you."

She asked other Christians to help him, too. They gave him toothbrushes, toothpaste, washcloths, shaving cream, and shampoo. Others baked cookies and sent him money. Everybody prayed for Rudy, and he was able to finish college.

His next step was to go to Southwestern Baptist Theological Seminary in Fort Worth, Texas. While he was going to the seminary, Jovita was praying that he would find the right wife. "Not just anybody," she said, "one who loves God and will take care of Rudy. Nobody took care of him as he grew up."

She was not pleased with a girl friend that he found. "Rudy, it hurts my heart to tell you, but I don't think that girl is the one you need. I love you so much. I'm afraid for you. But it's up to you. Jovita tried to explain the reason she felt that way. Rudy was hurt and did not write Jovita again while he was at the seminary.

After graduation, he sent Jovita a picture. He wrote this note: "To my dear sister for scolding. Loving you, Rudy."

Jovita continued praying for Rudy and his family. She told Rudy, "I prayed for my father many years before he became a Christian. I'll do the same for your father until he becomes a Christian." Because of Jovita's concern, Rudy's grandmother, aunt, sister, stepmother, and father became Christians. And Rudy was invited back home.

Rudy married a beautiful woman named Ruth. He pastored Hispanic Baptist churches in Dallas and Corpus Christi, Texas, before going to work for the American Bible Society.

Key to Happiness

Victory Outreach

Jovita did not marry. She said, "Courage is my companion. Such courage makes me aware of God in Christ. He knows my weakness and needs. I want to be free to serve Him. Helping someone else is my key to happiness."

Jovita's desire to help drug addicts came about because of her brother Mike. He dropped out of high school and began using drugs. Jovita said, "It hurt me so much." He was a drug addict for twenty years.

While under the influence of alcohol and drugs, Mike killed a man. His sentence was death. Jovita and her family helped him during this time, and his sentence was changed to life imprisonment.

Before Señora Galan died, she talked with Jovita about Mike. "I believe that Mike will become a Christian someday. Jovita, please take care of him."

"I will, Mama," Jovita promised. She never stopped praying for Mike.

When he finally got out of prison, Mike continued to use drugs. He wandered from place to place.

One night he was in Chicago. He went to a Christian

center because he was hungry and needed a place to sleep. He thought, "I'll just stay here tonight. I'll leave tomorrow." But Mike liked it at the center, and he stayed.

On Wednesday night, the director of the center said, "Everybody goes to church tonight." Mike mumbled, "I don't want to go. I'll stay here." The director repeated loudly, "Everybody goes! If you want to live here, you go to church."

Two other young men, called "brothers," were appointed to go with Mike and help and care for him. They sat with him during the service. Mike didn't hear much of the sermon, but during the singing, he became a Christian.

Mike was sent to Teen Challenge in Pennsylvania. He worked out on a range taking care of cows. He also finished high school and got an electronics degree in college.

He went to the seminary for six months of Christian training so that he could witness to other drug addicts in the streets. After finishing the seminary, Mike went to New York to the First Presbyterian Church. He became the director of youth.

Demetrio couldn't believe that his brother was a Christian. His sister went to New York to see for herself. She wrote Jovita, "I am mailing you a ticket. Come and see that Mike is a Christian."

"Thank you," Jovita said. "I don't have to go to New York to know that Mike is a Christian." She never doubted that it was true.

Mike began holding rallies and revivals. He went to San Antonio, and his family helped him with rallies. They put announcements on the radio and in the newspapers. Mike's testimony to drug addicts was, "The only cure is Christ."

Jovita said, "I wish we had a Baptist center for drug addicts. We have Baptist hospitals and schools. Why can't we have a Baptist drug addict center?" She talked about this with members of differing Baptist churches. No one thought it was possible to have such a center. No one would help.

Freddie Garcia [gar-SEE-ah] had wished for a drug ministry in San Antonio, too. He met Jovita through Mike and talked with her about some of his plans. She liked what she heard.

Jovita sold the family home that had been given to her. She used the money as a down payment on a house for drug addicts. She and her sister Angie helped Freddie Garcia find a building to buy in a section of town called

"Devil's Lap." They helped him clean out the rats and snakes. They named it Victory Outreach, and Freddie Garcia became the director.

Jovita worked with him for four years in her spare time. (Of course, her main work was still her kindergarten and church work.) She was concerned about the children who were drug addicts. She organized a children's worship service, and she trained leaders to teach Vacation Bible School at the center.

After Mike returned to Chicago, he preached in the Plaza. An addict passed by and heard Mike's testimony. He became a Christian, and Mike sent him to Victory Outreach in San Antonio.

After being at Victory Outreach for awhile, Angie paid a three-year scholarship for the man to get training. He now directs a center for drug addicts in Corpus Christi, Texas.

Money or Missions

After her mother's death, Jovita said, "I wonder if I still have brains to get some kind of nurse's training?"

"Now, it's too late to get an education," someone answered.

"It's never too late," Jovita said, "if you really want to." She enrolled in Saint Phillips College to train as a nurse's aide. She said, "Praise God! I got good grades!"

The school offered Jovita a scholarship to get more nurse's training. "We will give you your uniforms, books, and $40 a week," she was told. Later this training would help her earn a better salary.

Jovita was tempted to accept this scholarship. Angie and Lily urged her to accept it. They talked to her so much about it that Jovita got upset. "Back off!" she begged. "Don't push so hard."

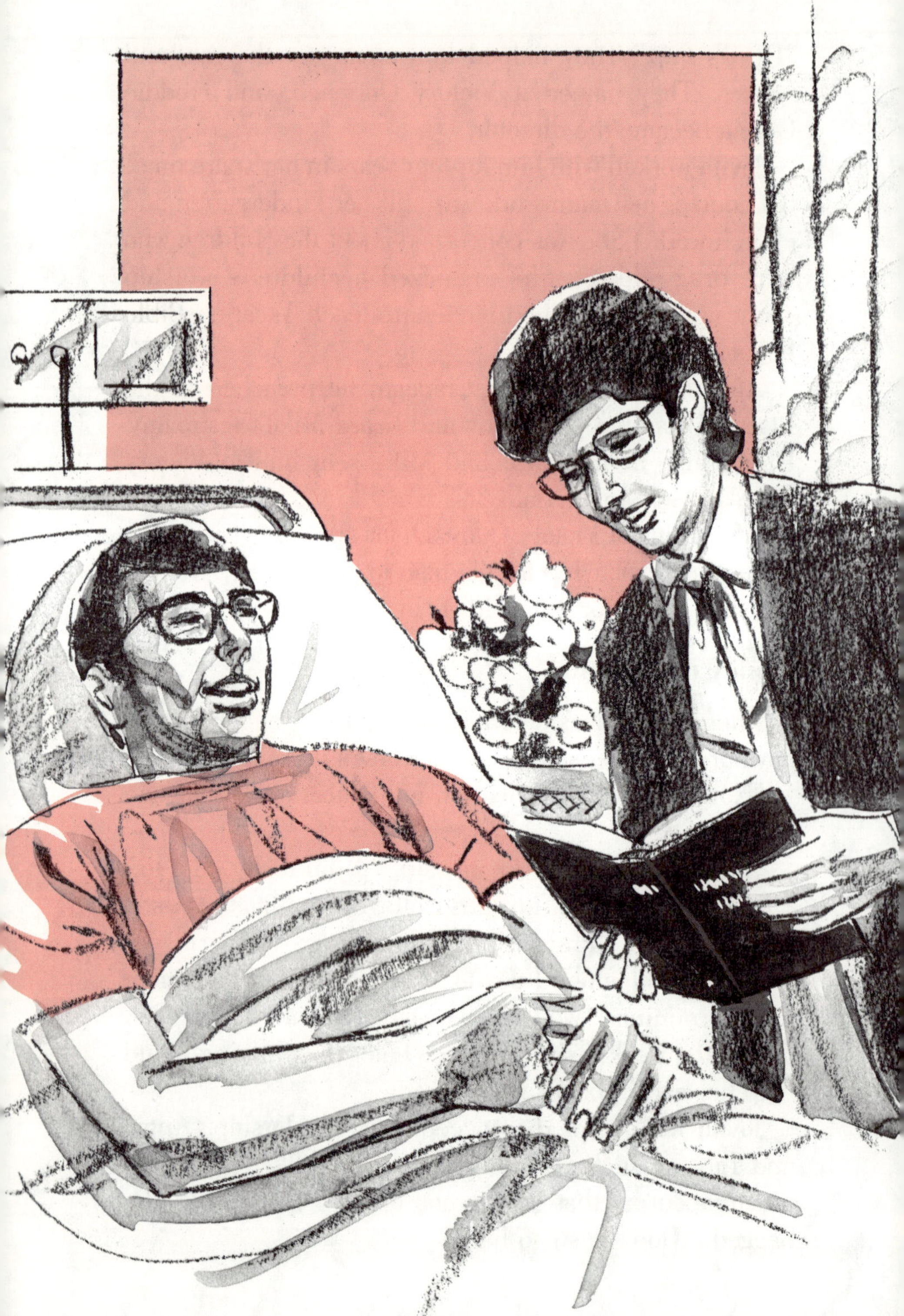

Finally, Jovita said, "No, if I accept this scholarship, I will have to give up being a home missionary. My mission work is first in my life. I'm not here for more degrees. I'm here to serve God." She cried, but she said, "I'm happy!"

Maybe it was partly because of her nurse's aide training that Jovita enjoyed visiting patients in the hospital. One patient she helped was Marcos Franco. He was unable to talk, so Jovita helped him learn to say his ABC's.

Señor Franco became a Christian, but he was unable to go to church. Jovita said, "Let's have prayer services in the home." She took her GA and Acteen members every week for a service.

One day Jovita said, "Let's change this. Let's take Baptist Women. They need to take this responsibility. The Acteen and GA members can do something else."

Baptist Women members began leading the prayer service for the seven to ten people who came every week. They used the Missionary prayer calendar and had Bible study. On other days, they visited in the neighborhood.

Acteen and GA members began helping Jovita at the Saint Benedict's Nursing Home.

Another patient Jovita helped was Mary Garcia. She had been in a car accident and lost a leg. Jovita visited her day after day in the hospital.

Later Jovita found a place for Mary and her family to live.

The Garcias had three children. Jovita helped with these children. She gave them their baths and washed their clothes.

After Mary got an artificial leg, Jovita helped her learn to walk.

One day Jovita visited Mary in her apartment. When

Mary came to the door, she was in her wheelchair. Jovita leaned down and hugged Mary. After talking for awhile in Spanish, Jovita suggested, "Let's read from the Bible."

She opened the Bible and read some of her favorite psalms. "Psalms always helped me during a crisis," Jovita said. "I know they will help you, too.

"Now, let's pray."

After the prayer, Mary looked up with tears in her eyes. "You have been like a mother to me," Mary said. "You are amazing. You have the Lord in your heart."

From time to time, Jovita had offers for better jobs in bigger churches. A better-paying job would mean she would have a larger place to live and other nice things. This could have been tempting to Jovita. Maria Sevilla, a co-worker, said, "She lived on a very strict budget. She ate only one meal a day, but if she saw that someone else needed to eat, she did without to help." But Jovita's first love was not money. It was her mission work—helping others. She said, "God has never failed me, and I promised to give my life to Him at any price."

One hot, sweltering summer day, Jovita was driving to Dallas, Texas. She had given up her vacation time to help in Vacation Bible School at Calvary Baptist Mission.

As she drove along, the air conditioner in the car broke. Jovita didn't have any money to pay for having it fixed. What could she do?

She prayed, "God, You know it's so hot, and I get terrible headaches in the heat. Keep me cool." And He did!

River Ministry

"Hello, is this Jovita Galan?" the voice on the telephone asked.

"Si [SEE—yes]," Jovita answered.

"This is Elmin Howell from the River Ministry Office in Dallas. We would like for you to help prepare material for preschoolers and to help us in training our preschool leaders."

Jovita knew about the Rio Grande River Ministry of Texas Baptists. Each winter, hundreds of volunteers were trained to help others. One workshop was offered entirely in Spanish, and Spanish-speaking people helped in the other workshops. The volunteers were trained in witnessing, music, medical ministries, puppets, and Vacation Bible School.

The volunteers used this training doing summer missionary work with Mexican-Americans who lived along the river. The Rio Grande River flows along the Texas-Mexico border for 890 miles. It passes through the homeland of three-and-one-half million people.

During the first year of this work two thousand people became Christians. Over five thousand Texas Baptists had volunteered to work. Some were farmers, nurses, school teachers, truck drivers, carpenters, and students. About 150 churches helped in mission Vacation Bible Schools and evangelism.

"Will you be able to help us?" Mr. Howell asked, interrupting Jovita's thoughts.

Jovita answered, "This is something else I can do to help someone. Si, I will help you."

She helped prepare two books for four- and five-year-olds. She taught singing in English and Spanish. She taught different ways to learn Bible memory verses.

Jovita worked with Mr. Howell for three years helping prepare for the River Ministry.

Unselfishness Continues

Apartment Bible Club

A month after Jovita became sixty-seven years old, she moved to an apartment. Her sister Angie didn't want her to move. "I want you to stay here close to me. Please don't move."

"Now, Angie," Jovita replied, "you know my home has been broken into several times. I have had two typewriters stolen. I will be safer in the new apartment."

After moving, Jovita was concerned about the people who lived in the other apartments. "I wonder what I can do to help them?" she asked herself. There were a total of ninety apartments in the complex.

She began visiting from door to door. When someone answered her knock Jovita said, "I would like to have a Bible Club in my apartment. Will you come?" Not all of them came, but many times eighteen to twenty women crowded into Jovita's small apartment.

She decided more publicity was needed. She had pamphlets printed that told about the Bible study. She paid for these herself. Afterwards when she visited, she always left a pamphlet as a reminder.

One day she knocked on a door. As a woman opened

the door, Jovita said, *"Como esta, hermana* [COH-moh ehs-TAH air-MAH-nah—How do you do, sister]. I'm Jovita Galan."

"Como esta," the woman answered. "I'm Lily Lara."

"I have a Bible club in my apartment every week. Will you come?" Jovita asked Lily.

"Si," Lily answered. She began attending every week and helping Jovita every day. She visited the sick in the apartments and brought a report to Jovita. If Lily felt that Jovita needed to see someone because of her nurse's aide training, Jovita would go and check on the person.

"We need to pray for people," Jovita said. So she organized a prayer group among the women in the apartment complex. "You do the praying," she told them. "Lily and I will do the doing."

When a member of the prayer group had a birthday, Jovita's apartment was too small for everyone to come. She paid fifty dollars of her own money each time to rent a meeting room in the apartment complex. She had to make sure that it was left "spick and span" after the meeting.

When Lily had a birthday, Jovita asked her to stand up and come to the front of the room. "We're so poor, we couldn't buy you a gift," Jovita said. "But we have a surprise for you." Each woman came by and pinned a one-dollar bill on Lily's dress. "Now you can buy your own gift," Jovita laughingly told her. Everyone had so much fun, they continued doing this for every member's birthday.

One day a man came up to Jovita. "I'm Raymon Zapata [zah-PAH-tah]. I understand you have a meeting in your apartment."

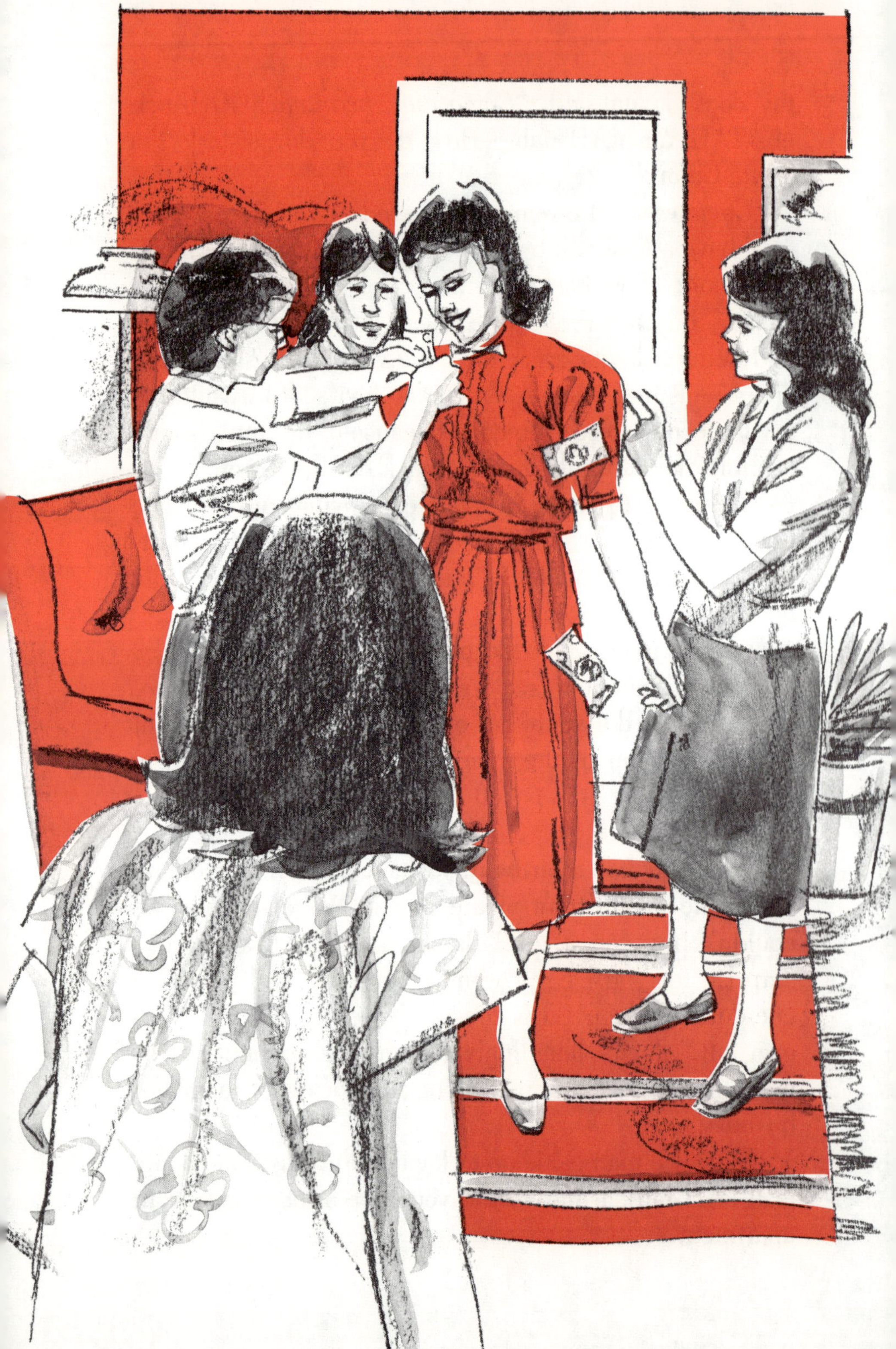

"*Si*," Jovita answered.

"You don't have men?" Raymon asked.

"No," Jovita explained. "It's too crowded. We are elbow to elbow when eighteen people come."

"Would you please help me to organize a group called Al-Anon? Do you know that organization?" Raymon continued.

"Yes, Raymon, I know about Al-Anon, the organization of alcoholics—people who have a drinking problem. I'd be more than glad to help you!"

They continued talking and wondered about a place to meet. They decided that a church would be the best place. Jovita said, "There's a church across the railroad. Why don't we ask the church if we can meet in their building?"

"You go and talk and come and tell me," Raymon suggested. He continued, "I don't want to drink. Do you know why I go to the cantina (kahn-TEE-nah—a drinking place)? To have some men to talk to. We are lonely!"

Jovita went to the church across the railroad. She introduced herself to the pastor and asked if the men could meet in the church.

"Well, I'm new here," the pastor replied, "and I understand that Al-Anon members smoke. I don't know if the people would like that."

"Please talk to them," Jovita said as she left. She thought, "My church is so far, I would have to take the men in my car if we met there. My car is small and only has two doors. I can't put every man in there. What can I do?"

During the next few weeks, Jovita began making a list of other places that might be used for the Al-Anon meetings. She thought about seeing if the hospital had a room that they could use. She thought about writing a letter to the apartment manager asking permission to let them use the meeting room free.

Before she could do any of these things, Raymon was killed in an accident. "I will not quit!" Jovita said. "I will continue to try to help these lonely men who are alcoholics."

The apartment Bible club was not Jovita's fulltime job. She was no longer teaching kindergarten, but she continued all her other church activities.

Jovita worked at the church office four hours every day. She led jail and hospital ministries. She was still active in Woman's Missionary Union.

Instead of retiring on her seventieth birthday on February 15, 1985, Jovita was appointed by the Home Mission Board to work another year. She moved to a larger apartment. Right away, she started a new Bible study.

Dream for the Future

"I would like to use my nursing experience and work at a hospital in Guadalajara (gwahd-ah-lah-HAH-rah), Mexico. This is my dream," said Jovita to a friend. "I would like to talk and visit with patients."

Jovita explained that a friend named Kay was working in Guadalajara. The friend told Jovita she must pass a test in order to work at the hospital.

"I may try to do that," Jovita said. "Or, I may just go on my own and say 'Here I am—use me!'"

"If I don't use my nursing training," Jovita continued, "I will try to find a Spanish-speaking church with a need for a volunteer worker. I will pay my own expenses. I will ask only for a room to sleep."

She explained that she would like to help the church with Woman's Missionary Union organizations and Bible clubs. She would like to visit people to invite them to church. She would like to train workers.

Jovita's Prayer

Four days before Jovita was seventy years old, she entertained a visitor in her apartment. They laughed and talked together. Jovita played the piano and then decided to serve refreshments. As she bustled about the kitchen in her energetic way mixing orange juice, she said: "I pray the Lord to let me live as long as I'm able to do His work. If the day comes when I'm unable to do, I want to go home and rest."

Amarillo
Dallas
Ft. Worth
El Paso
San Angelo
San Antonio
Pearsall
Corpus
Christi
Alice
Torreón
Guadalajara
Mexico City

Remember

What was the miracle in Mexico? Why did this happen?
What were the secret stories Señora Galan told her children?
When did Jovita hear the Bible read for the first time and begin going to church?
Where was Jovita when she promised to serve God?
What work did Jovita do when she was appointed a home missionary?
What other church work did she do?
What was Jovita's key to happiness?
Why do you think Jovita was called "God's unselfish servant"?
Think of a time when Jovita was
 —unselfish with her time.
 —unselfish with her money.
 —unselfish with her car.
 —unselfish with her home.
Think of some ways that you can be unselfish
 —to your family.
 —to your friends.
 —to your neighbors.

About the Author

Lou Sherrill is a home missionary. She lives in Bismarck, North Dakota, with her husband Tom. They work in the western half of the state of North Dakota. As WMU president for the Northern Plains Baptist Convention, Lou works with ladies from North Dakota, South Dakota, and Montana. She has written study material to help girls learn about missions.